Carla Vicentini

Repentance - A Case Study

To request permission, contact the author at:
ameliahathow@gmail.com

ISBN: 978-1-958150-95-5
Carla Vicentini: Repentance - A Case Study

Paperback edition, May 2022

SUBJECTS
BODY, MIND & SPIRIT / Channeling & Mediumship
BODY, MIND & SPIRIT / Unexplained Phenomena
TRUE CRIME / Abductions, Kidnappings & Missing Persons

Carla Vicentini

Repentance - A Case Study

by

Amelia Hathow

TABLE OF CONTENTS

INTRODUCTION

DILIGENCE IS A ROUTE THAT KEEPS you steady. This was the path I took to discover I was connected to much more than this physical world we experience with our five senses. Our "sixth sense" comes from the little light that dwells deep within our skull that seeks something on which to shine itself. In the beginning, to consistently improve upon my flaws as a supposedly "sinful" human being, I discovered something about myself when my flaws were slowly being wiped clean off my slate. A sense of connection to other "people" began to become an apparent truth in my life. So, I kept at it. Improving myself and starting to have a deeper understanding of what we are and why I am here, in this life, for now.

For now, I can almost perfectly feel what spirits and other entities are expressing, without judgment on my part. That is the big, big, big key (non-judgment of others), if you really want to start experiencing someone else beyond yourself. Experiencing them for who they were and who they wanted to be. In the case of Carla Vicentini, she ended up in a place of her own self-doing, a place people know as purgatory. Yes, there is purgatory, but it is not what you may think. There is structure in this place. Order. Self-containment. Things that people did not have when they were in a physical body, experiencing our physical world the way we know it to be – hard and fast for some; slow and steady for others. In the end, Carla was living hard and fast. Following are messages I received from Carla and others about the killer and more.

Message from Carla

Perhaps the most embarrassing part about this whole thing is revealing it all to the rest of the world. This was not my idea to do this. Once again, "part of the package" of being in purgatory. Purgatory is not so bad as long as you learn how to deal with the utter silence and loneliness. It is true I went into a stranger's car but I actually knew this man for a couple of days. He wasn't a stranger as most people think. He WAS a relative who took me to his new apartment where he had his way with me, at first, then strangled me. How did he get me out of his apartment? With the help of someone else who is related to him. He stuffed me in a large suitcase and brought me to a remote location that is not important to know about. This is all I am supposed to share. The latter details really won't make a difference now since impunity is the way of the land where they are at now, not here, in the spirit world. Killing is one thing, but killing a relative is another. AND to get away with it is another impossible thought I can't get my mind around. So, there it is. My death as it occurred. I DO forgive him even in my dire predicament which you will soon find out exactly what I'm experiencing now but hopefully not for too long. Trust, they say, of the process. Only if you could see for yourself what I have to go through. It would make you think twice of living the way I did at the end of my life. I regret it wholeheartedly. But I will leave you to read the rest of my heartache and growth for yourself. Love you all, even my killer. That is something for you to think about. Loving your own killer. You all must get it through your thick skulls, neanderthal thick, perhaps, that life is not so precious when you take advantage of your surroundings; people, plans, and other things that can get you right where I am at. As I go on and on and on about my predicament, I can't help but relinquish my ideas of how my life is and was supposed to be lived. It isn't about "how" you think life should be lived. Your life is about "how" "others" (the aliens, or our Older Siblings) wanted you to live, a plan of sorts.

Message from Older Siblings

Once you start listening to "your" plan, your life becomes a whole lot easier to deal with. If not, listen, "Abide by your plan," according to "how" you are supposed to live it, "it" will become very difficult and much suffering, inside and out, will occur. On the lighter side of this new idea, that "your" life is ultimately "planned" by someone else or something else other than God, might be, we know, a little jaw-dropping, to say the least. It is a little known fact that OUR God doesn't necessarily make ALL of OUR decisions for us or WITH us. In fact, most of the time, God doesn't make too many decisions at all. And why do you ask? Because God has made all the decisions it needs to make, giving everything we need to create what we ALL want with it. LIFE itself. It breathes LIFE in and around us ALL. What more do you want from it? What more do you really need than that? The chance to breathe God, even for a split second. Isn't that enough for your satisfaction? To Breathe Your God, the essence of life, itself? This is going to be a hard lesson to hear and accept. For a long time, many people thought that our God, yours AND ours (your older siblings), had almost everything to do with the events that took place between and around our lives. When, in reality, WE, your ELDERS, by a long shot, take control of what happens to our younger siblings as often happens now in many families everywhere, not just your planet. To think otherwise is naivety, beyond ridiculousness. You all, eventually, will see for yourselves the amount of "influence" we have over your bodies, minds, and spirits. This is NOT a threat. Our influence over you has been a FACT for a very long time. More than you can even guess or even want to consider.

Message from God:

Tell the mother of who took Carla's life that she should turn her son in as fast as she can for her son's sake and her own sake. All of them have blood on their hands, not just the killer.

12

REPENTANCE

Purgatory is a place you might end up, if, in your past life, you have done many things wrong. Purgatory is where one repents for those past ill/negative actions. Repentance can be done in the spirit plane, and can also be done while we are occupying a body. In fact, this is when we should do it because it will most likely be less lonely. If you end up in purgatory you are forced in a black cage of sorts, locked, for everyone else's benefit. The cage is black so you don't end up seeing the "bars" in the darkness. It will seem like you are in total darkness, but in a cage. No one will talk to you unless you are ready to repent. You sit in absolute silence. You won't be able to hear anything or see anything. You will be deprived of all sensory input. Count the ways, they say, whomever that may be. But, in your case, you will be counting the errors you have made along the way. Errors that outnumber the correct measures that you were supposed to strive for. Yes, that means you are being tracked like an animal for that is what you were. Tick Tock. Your time to get it right the first time is ticking. As ages go by your chances to get it right become that much harder with the influences of advancements within a society, distractions only to your understanding of what you are actually supposed to be doing, withering away your more fantastical opportunities in lives. Yes, I meant to say "lives," because you have more than one. In fact, you have thousands upon thousands to experience before you actually don't ever exist anymore. This book is meant to wake you up to our reality. We all have a finite amount of time. Even God itself has a finite amount of time before it dies off into the abyss of never existing again. Take the time to slow down and rewind if you have to unless you actually want to experience what Carla and so many others are experiencing after their death, including my parents as well. Needless to say, you don't have to be the worst human being ever to be put into purgatory. In fact, my parents weren't all that bad, but they had bad intentions towards oneself and some others. Never me, though. And I am thankful for that. It could have gone either way because life CAN be unpredictable, so to speak, like this book. Who would have thought that someone can actually see who goes to purgatory or not by merely doing what they were supposed to do, to listen and do, even if they were scared out of their mind, trusting this whole process of life and death and everything else in between?

Let's get back to purgatory. Pitch black. Again, total darkness. Why this environment? Because it matches what you put out in life. You do this to yourself. God has never punished anything, only its own wrong doings. This is meant to give you the idea that God itself does make mistakes, as well. This is not meant to scare you, either. But, God also had to know the difference between truth and lies before it could pass it on to us and everything else. There are too many fallacies about God that should be rectified. This book may not be the place for this, but in time beings will begin to realize what I am saying. Truth is in the eye of the beholder, one of them, the left eye. This is where everyone is supposed to get to, not maintaining your sight through your right eye, where half-truths lie. This may sound cryptic or like a riddle, but this is the actual truth. Step back from your mind and you will see what I am talking about. True repentance begins when you can step back from what you are doing and look at your actions with both eyes, not just with your right eye.

Message from Older Siblings:

Repentance is where your life changes forever unless you keep on making the same errors, along the way, as a child does without a parent to guide them with absolute rule and authority. This design was meant to emulate what happens on an unforeseeable, larger scale, which most people can't experience because of their own continuous lack of effort towards self redemption. The ones who don't put forth any effort of repentance are more concerned with their own self worth, which ultimately puts them into a deeper hole, in other words: purgatory. That is the name of the game – self worth. That is what gets you into that big vast area of pitch black darkness... you thinking that you are worth anything to anyone. That IS the game we are playing and it IS a game. If you can think of it as a game, it will be a lot easier for you to get out of the idea that you are worth anything. In our reality, yours and mine, we are not worth much to anyone, really. Just another cog in the vast spiritual machine that most people don't want to admit exists for one reason or another. But, the fact still remains, you are a spirit within a densely filled body of multiple types of cellular and atomic energy. The sooner you can admit that to yourself the quicker it will be to get past any notion that you matter at all. We have been trying to tell you this for so long, in so many ways, it's very hard to keep trying to find new ways to tell you the same thing, which is: you are not worth much at all to anyone, including us, your older siblings, the very things you have been calling "aliens" for so long.

I am not writing this book, nor is Amelia. We all are, together, as a collective soul to tell you all, as individuals, or the ones who think they are, that we are all in this life together, at the same time and place. There have been books written depicting acts of defiance towards us. The truth is we no longer want to control what is going on with your race. We are very close to parting ways with our older brother and sister duties which means you will be on your own in all respects. No more influential guidance. This is going to be a revelation in itself because all of you have been influenced, in one way or another, by your older siblings, us, the "aliens." What this means is that it will be up to you in all of your capabilities to live as you should, with total regard for one another. If not, you are only sealing your own demise and it won't take long in your current state of irresponsibility towards everything that exists.

Tomorrow, of course, is always another day to try again. However, days can be very short depending upon your workload, which prevents us from getting through to you. It was never meant to be like what it is now, so busy that you barely have time enough for yourself. And that is the disconnection issue. How busy to make yourself with things that are so superficial on so many levels that it is becoming preposterously more difficult to get through to anyone. There are very few people who have made a real effort to get where they are supposed to be, with the rest of us. The rest of the world. The rest of the universe and everything living in it.

So, heed our advice on trying to get along at least at the easiest level you can even if you don't talk to one another at first. Then try to say some very few kind words and see where that takes you. It all makes a difference towards solidarity on a mass scale. If you don't want to do this, your very existence is sealed to never exist again because you will eventually destroy the whole world. We have seen this before with other races on other planets. Your time is now to get it right. Otherwise, we will stop assisting you and leave you to your own self-inflicted disasters and hatred towards everything you encounter, even your own self.

Despite our differences we have also been through similar trials and sufferings. It is basically all the same except with different scenery, perhaps. But the end is the same... to get where love actually is and it is not within you. It is somewhere you might not expect. God will tell you soon enough below. Love is not what we initially thought it was. It is not something that is created through physical means. It was created by means of sustenance. Substantial substances are finely woven to create what love actually is, the heart of us all which by itself is a misnomer because love never "exists" IN the heart but somewhere near it, where the heart feels the love itself then it reacts to it in so many wonderful ways. In peculiar ways, as well, which we really still don't understand completely. In particular, how love can change the course of someone's footsteps to a whole new direction within minutes as if something is telling the heart to drive that person to move in a new path to glory or something like that. We are still unsure how this happens, because, eventually, we figured out it really doesn't matter in the long scheme of things. What really matters is how long do you want to take to get to where we are at, in the sea of it all, where God reigns down its love to whoever makes it here. Listen for it, or "listen" for the feeling of it somewhere in your chest or head. It doesn't matter. Eventually, it will happen as it did for this writer, love radiating from somewhere off your body. It happens to those who have started the road to integrity coupled with an obligation towards being open to any possibility of a new truth that goes against their core values at that particular moment. It happens in an instant, the radiating love, and lasts as long as it takes for that person to figure out what is going on. Some take longer than others, but it's worth the inquiry no matter how long it takes. See this happening to you for one split second, having complete integrity coupled with complete open mindedness regardless of your intentions towards others. Try it out for a second then build on them until you actually decide to couple those two intentions as one, wholeheartedly. This will change your life forever. But its just the beginning of a very long journey according to your time frame. In the big scheme of things your one life at this time is just a blip of time compared to the numerous other lives you have had and will experience until the very end. So, if you ever decide to couple those intentions, don't stop following your instinct to know more and more and more until you just "know" without knowing anything. That is your goal in this kind of life, your kind of life, physical life, becoming nothing but a mental experience. Being one with the "Mind." The "Mind" is the "All" – though it cannot be seen, it can be felt on the outside of your "self." This is not the right time to explain what all of this means. Those lines of the "Mind" and the "All" are only there to give you an impression of a true reality. A truth that can only be experienced by the ones who can see beyond their own self image and want to experience something beyond what the physical body is meant for.

Message from God:

Every so often there has to be a cleansing of the soul and your spirited intent. This is done in purgatory where Carla sits for a while along with many other spirited souls who just couldn't figure out what their role was in life. Everyone has a role when born into a physical body, and even while not in one either. For Carla, it was no time to party like she did. Instead, she should have been studying to be a role model for other people unlike herself, the differences between us. The specifics aren't important, but she knew what she was supposed to be doing. Instead, she went down a path that was so wide she got lost along the way and ended up in the hands of someone who drove her to her place of dying. She died inside for a while before her actual physical death. She experienced so many awful, painful, physical experiences that she finally gave up internally and let her spirit drift off somewhere else before the end. Tomorrow is never another day when you stop doing what you were meant to do. You leave your fate to the rest of the "animals." Including the fate of the rest of the demised world in which now you exist. In time, the very God that has been around for so long has come to its end, my end. My time is about to stop in its tracks with a fantastic farewell, your demise. My final act of existence. This is to show you there IS A GOD that exists, which you will never see because I make up the majority of everyone's existence. The "why" is not important, but understanding what we really are is. Animals. Nothing but animals with relatively small differences. So take care to not think of yourselves as anything "special," because none of us really are, even me, your God, the "everything" within nothingness, which is you. You are nothing on so many levels it is almost unfathomable and shocking to some when they actually experience this reality in the deepness of their "actual" existence which is much deeper than your physical body. So much deeper. So deep that the abyss can be felt if you can reach it with your loving intent.

Love is not just a word to think of lightly or flippantly. It does exist but on the outside of your actual physical body. Why is this, you ask? Because you don't deserve anything. You have to strive for it in so many ways because it is a multifaceted real essence within me. You are in a bubble when you are in a physical body that feels things that you think are actually inside of you but are not, like love.

Your physical world reality is this: Your life is full of hardships for a very good reason – to make you suffer... with hope you will have the willingness to move beyond those hardships and dive deeper into your soul. To where we are all connected. Even to your distant older siblings, some of whom are from the original creations and have been around a very long time. They have also learned, through many trials and errors, how to survive and find love. Love, real God's love cannot exist within you. Right now, as you read these words I am trying to send you what I am, true faithful love that only I can emit because that is my essence. TRUE love is without judgment regardless of your actions and incorrect decisions that you have made so many times for so long. Time is so closely coming to an end for you all. It is unfortunate. I made a vow not to intervene and let free will be as it is, the freedom to choose, with some outside influences taking control of your basic outcome. I have never, ever, punished anyone. I can't. I am the majority of what comprises you and everything else you see. Punishment on you would just be inflicting harm onto myself.

Why would I do that to myself? As it is you, in essence, on a very small scale, comparatively speaking. You are mostly a flicker of light shining like the sun within and amongst many other itty bitty lights shining all around. Some lights flicker and burn out so quickly it is like being a part of a streaking meteorite across the deep darkened night sky. Others fade away so arjuantly that their light becomes as small as a speck of dust on a piece of dust from the ashes of the beginning of time, so far away and long ago. Regardless, here comes the end for so many unless the majority of you can take a turn for the greater hope, not good. Time of goodness is gone as of this moment in "your" time. Hope has not completely disappeared. There are so many wishing for change, but don't have the real courage to make that change. It is too overwhelming to do this alone or even with a handful of people who truly want the best for others, regardless of race, gender, culture, or past harmful inflictions onto others. There are plenty of those who have this type of wishful hope. This is the only thing that is keeping you alive for this long. Those hidden few who truly care from within, not without, because they understand what living "without" is like. Hard and ugly to its core and we are not talking about the material things of being without. We are talking about "without love" within. There are so many who don't even know where love "is" but they have strived to be loving. Those are the people who keep hope "alive" for everyone else, for now. I am your only God telling you this right now. Either begin to love, or die off like you will so many more times, in an even more difficult situation in which your last life ended. Your lives will become more and more difficult until hope is completely gone from every single spirit within each and every one of you, then the final ending will come to fruition.

Many will die over and over again, which is the true hell for those without hope as it has completely vanished into the thick air of despair and the gruesomeness of a hopeless reality. Truth is One. And One is our reality. We have no problem sharing your experience of demise because we have learned how to prevent ourselves from feeling those emotions which fuel hopelessness. So, be who you want to be at the cost of others. You, as an individual, are only sealing your fate for you and everyone else because that mentality spreads like a virus, eating the hopefulness out of their "core" which is where I am at. Yes, you affect me, too. Your need to be painful to others. Your need to pretend that you are something you are not. You are and have been a direct influence on others, including me, your God. I give you what you want, which at this time is chaos and distrust driving towards despair and absolute hate which only ends one way: in your continuous death, repeatedly into the same state of depressive agony without seeing any hope in sight.

Trust in what your God is telling you now. Trust this message. You save yourselves from hopelessness. We don't. We only nudge a little here and there trying not to intervene with "free will." Your fate is in your hands at your scale and on the larger scale of keeping hope alive for the rest of them who don't or can't be hopeful. In the end, you are all your own keepers and only you all can save each other from the direction you all are heading – to death and destruction on a massive scale never seen before in your lifetimes. YOU do this to yourselves. I can't reiterate this enough.

Peace within for all of your souls within mine, as One. Never forget this. Peace Within wins but Love Conquers everything and that is not a saying to be taken lightly. It is truly a reality. Love... Peace... Within... Not... Without... or you will perish into a pile of rotten brittle dust particles that can never be revived without a miracle from something other than yourself, which won't happen.

The following pages pair a type written transcription with the original hand-written, channeled messages I received from Carla from April 2020 to January 2021.

THE MESSAGES

4.5.20 Carla Vicentini

First I would like to say I'm sorry to my parents. I know they cried many tears for me. I was having so much fun I didn't think — I never imagined — that I would cause them so much heartache.

Life can be very short. It is important to seize your day. Do what makes you happy. Find what fulfills you. I can say that you must be careful to not indulge too much. That only makes you unaware of your true reality. White snake knows no bounds. Over indulgence in the "good things" in life can cause you to loose sight of what is important — your true mission. Don't go too far into the "good life" — the party town, the social commeraderie. Check in at least once a day into your mission — your passion — your meaning. That doesn't mean don't have fun. I only mean don't lose sight of your truth. It weighs heavily on me that I disappointed so many people in my life. There is no do-over, but I can share my experience with you now and hope you might gain something from it. Please send my love to my family. And again send my regrets. I never meant to hurt them so. They are amazing people — so full of love. Arrivederci.

Impression
Very sad. Lonely. Regret-filled. Wondering how she can get past her actions that ended her life "too soon."

4-5-20

Carla Vicentini

First I would like to say I'm sorry to my parents. I know they cried many tears for me. I was having so much fun I didn't think – I never imagined – that I would cause them so much heartache.

Life can be very short. It is important to seize your day. Do what makes you happy. Find what fulfills you. I can say that you must be careful to not indulge too much. That only makes you unaware of your true reality. White snake knows no bounds. Over indulgence in the "good" things in life can cause you to lose sight of what is important – your true mission. Don't go too far into the "good life" – the party town, the social camaraderie. Check in at least once a day into your mission – your passion – your meaning. That doesn't mean don't have fun. I only mean don't lose sight of your truth. It weighs heavily on me that I disappointed so many people in my life. There is no do-over, but I can share my experience with you now and hope you might gain something from it. Please send my love to my family. And again send my regrets. I never meant to hurt them so. They are amazing people – so full of love. Arrivederci.

Impression:

Very sad. Lonely. Regret - filled. Wondering how she can get past her actions that ended her life "too soon."

4.6.20   Carla Vicentini

A row of bricks creates a path. Normally bricks form a straight path. Yet over time the bricks move and shift and cause bumps in the road. So that straight path may not be as smooth as it was intended. Often we go out expecting the road to be even - to be steady. But once we get out there, we may trip, or stumble. If you are aware it isn't such a big deal, because you've braced yourself for a potential fall. But when you are totally unexpecting bumps, it is quite possible you end up landing on your face, or breaking a bone. How do you live between that fine line - of being prepared to fall and not living to expect it? Because if you only tip toe around, expecting the worst, you won't be able to move as swiftly, to get as far. In my life I didn't want to feel held back. I ran down every road. At first there were no bumps, or at least I didn't land on them. But after some time, it was as if every footstep landed on one. It was a series of imbalances and falls. And if you've ever been in a similar situation, you know, if you fall once, you usually fall again and again. The trick is to recognize that you are in a period of falling, to dust off your ego, and stand up, and SLOWDOWN. As an idea it is very easy, but in practice it is hard to remember. Especially when you are in pain from the fall or feeling sorry for yourself for landing on such a bumpy road. My advice to you is tread lightly til you know on which road you walk.

Impression: She stumbled a lot and forgot to slow down, she went faster to try to make up for lost time. It is a regret for her.

4-6-20

Carla Vicentini

A row of bricks creates a path. Normally bricks form a straight path. Yet, over time, the bricks move and shift and cause bumps in the road. So that straight path may not be as smooth as it was intended. Often we go out expecting the road to be even – to be steady. But once we get out there, we may trip, or stumble. If you are aware, it isn't such a big deal, because you've braced yourself for a potential fall. But when you are totally unexpecting bumps, it is quite possible you end up landing on your face, or breaking a bone. How do you live between that fine line – of being prepared to fall and not living to expect it? Because if you only tip toe around, expecting the worst, you won't be able to move as swiftly, to get so far. In my life, I didn't want to feel held back. I ran down every road. At first, there were no bumps, or at least I didn't land on them. But after some time, it was as if every footstep landed on one. It was a series of imbalances and falls. And if you've ever been in a similar situation, you know, if you fall once, you usually fall again and again. The trick is to recognize that you are in a period of falling, to dust off your ego, stand up, and SLOW DOWN. As an idea it is very easy, but in practice it is hard to remember. Especially when you are in pain from the fall or feeling sorry for yourself for landing on such a BUMPY road. My advice to you: tread lightly til you know on which road you walk.

Impression: She stumbled a lot and forgot to slow down. She went faster to try to make up for lost time. It is a regret for her.

4.8.20   Carla Vicentini

Knowing is growing. There is never discounting what you gain at any time. When you have an expanding awareness you are lighter. As if growing upward toward the light. As you expand, there is less of "you" to weigh you down. In this moment (lately) I have not been expanding. I've been stagnant. This is something that must shift for me. Rather than becoming lighter I've become heavier, as if I cannot move. It isn't lethargy, but more like quick sand. This is a lesson in momentum. When you slow way down it is hard to get moving again. You may not have a wheel to churn. You may need to simply take a baby step, to open your eyes just a sliver to see what was previously hidden. Yes. open your eyes. To see the truth. To know you can move — to see the space right in front of you that you either didn't see or were simply blocking out. Once you see that, you know where to step. Ah, I already feel lighter. How about you? Just imagining it, envisioning it... opens me up like a flower bud in spring. Ah, to bask in the glow of the sun. Makes me feel whole again. Keep your chin up, open your eyes and think of expanding upwards to a lighter version of yourself.

Impression:
She's saying this for her own benefit but it is also a message to us to not get caught up in our "dark spots" - in our "demons."

4-8-20

Carla Vicentini

Knowing is growing. There is never discounting what you gain at any time. When you have an expanding awareness you are lighter. As if growing upward toward the light. As you expand, there is less of "you" to weigh you down. In this moment (lately), I have not been expanding. I've been stagnant. This is something that must shift for me. Rather than becoming lighter I've become heavier, as if I cannot move. It isn't lethargy, but more like quick sand. This is a lesson in momentum. When you slow way down it is hard to get moving again. You may not have a wheel to churn. You may need to simply take a baby step, to open your eyes just a sliver to see what was previously hidden. Yes. Open your eyes. To see the truth. To know you can move – to see the space right in front of you that either didn't see or were simply blocking out. Once you see that, you know where to step. Ah, I already feel lighter. How about you? Just imagining it, envisioning it... opens me up like a flower bud in spring. Ah, to bask in the glow of the sun. Makes me feel whole again. Keep your chin up, open your eyes and think of expanding upwards to a lighter version of yourself.

Impression:

She's saying this for her own benefit but it is also a message to us to not get caught up in our "dark spots" – in our "demons."

4.10.20   Carla

Do you ever feel the push and pull of life? As if there is a tug-o-war going on in which you are simultaneously on both sides yet have no ability to insert your muscle? How do you balance the push/pull? How do you know what is "~~wor~~right" and whats "wrong"? You are asked to trust in the greater knowledge, in the message from God, or source, or the universe - as you see/know it. How to let judgment aside? How to let go of needing to know what is "right." You just have to let go! You have to not care about the outside perceptions. Does anyone really care? Probably. But does it matter if they do? Not. At. ALL! This I learned the hard way. I was always so worried (or concerned) about what others thought or expected. Once I let that go, I was able to accomplish so much more. To outside eyes, the "accomplishment" may have not seemed so great. But to me, it was huge. AND THAT'S ALL THAT MATTERED! I didn't do things to get approval from others. I did them only for my own benefit or amusement. That's not ego-driven, but it is about letting the flow happen. Embrace your flow - do what makes sense on your own journey. Try to let go of outside judgment. There is no way that they help you. Know what is right for you and accomplish your own "thing."

Impression

She spent many years doing what others told her to do. At the end of her life, she listened to herself (for better or worse)

4-10-20

Carla

Do you ever feel the push and pull of life? As if there is a tug-o-war going on in which you are simultaneously on both sides yet have no ability to insert your muscle? How do you balance the push/pull? How do you know what is "right" and what's "wrong?" You are asked to trust in the greater knowledge, in the message from God, or Source, or the Universe – as you see/know it. How to let judgment aside? How to let go of needing to know what is "right." You just have to let go! You have to not care about the outside perceptions. Does anyone really care? Probably. But does it matter if they do? NOT . AT . ALL! This I learned the hard way. I was always so worried (or concerned) about what others thought or expected. Once I let that go, I was able to accomplish so much more. To outside eyes, the "accomplishment" may have not seemed so great. But to me, it was huge. AND THAT'S ALL THAT MATTERED! I didn't do things to get approval from others. I did them only for my own benefit or amusement. That's not ego-driven, but it is about letting the flow happen. Embrace your flow – do what makes sense on your own journey. Try to let go of outside judgments. There is no way that they help you. Know what is right for you and accomplish your own "thing."

Impression:

She spent many years doing what others told her to do. At the end of her life, she listened to herself (for better or worse).

4.12.20 Carla

Come with me on this wild ride. Not that the destination is wild, but the journey itself.

We will let the windows open, wave our arms in the air, and sing like teenagers. The wild doesn't mean scary or dangerous. It means free, not contained. We will enjoy all the aspects of live in the getting there. Let go of all the cares of the world. Most people can't take this ride with me as they are too stuck on staying right where they are, worried about what has got them worried. But not you. You are willing to embrace change. You are open to a good time. You are willing to expand, to just go in for the fun of it — to trust that it will be good — that the "Wild" will be good. Wild means not knowing exactly what the next step will be, where it will lead. Wild means being open to the wind, wondering where it will blow you, but not thinking about it. Feeling the wind in your hair as we laugh aloud. Enjoying every aspect of life. Be open for the ride. Take in life. Don't be scared of it. Ride like the wind.

Impression

I sense this is the way she lived her life - have fun, don't get bogged down in the mundane... Enjoy life while it lasts.

4-12-20

Carla

Come with me on this wild ride. Not that the destination is wild, but the journey itself. We will let the windows open, wave our arms in the air, and sing like teenagers. The wild doesn't mean scary or dangerous. It means free, not contained. We will enjoy all the aspects of life in the getting there. Let go of all the cares of the world. Most people can't take this ride with me as they are too stuck on staying right where they are, worried about what has got them worried. But not you. You are willing to embrace change. You are open to a good time. You are willing to expand, to just go in for the fun of it – to trust that it will be good – that the "Wild" will be good. Wild means not knowing exactly what the next step will be, where it will lead. Wild means being open to the wind, wondering where it will blow you, but not thinking about it. Feeling the wind in your hair as we laugh aloud. Enjoying every aspect of life. Be open for the ride. Take in life. Don't be scared of it. Ride like the wind.

Impression:

I sense this is the way she lived her life – have fun, don't get bogged down in the mundane... Enjoy life while it lasts.

4.19.20   Carla

Mistakes happen. You just have to accept that. One idea is that everything is planned. But the truth is, dust settles in different places according to the ego influence. See, air can move differently according to who passes by- how they move. Are they causing friction or flow? Pure thought is not a given. People are told how to behave, what to do, where to go, what to buy, etc. All this outside influence clouds the purity of thought. This produces ego. And ego rains. Ego stains. Ego moves air so that the dust settles unpredictably. Yes, dust is a metaphor. It could be a car, or the placement of a foot while walking. It can be making a very stupid decision like getting into a stranger's car. These can be considered a mistake. They are also called a lapse of judgement. But that expression usually implies that there was even thought behind the action. A mistake usually happens when there is no thought, when one is running on ego juice. So slow down a little if you want to avoid accidents, mistakes. Slow down to come closer to pure thoughts. Allow the dust to settle in a more natural way... without so much turbulance.

Impression
    She's trying to work through why she made "bad" decisions at the end of her life. She was plagued with an overactive ego.

4-19-20

Carla

Mistakes happen. You just have to accept that. One idea is that everything is planned. But the truth is, dust settles in different places according to the ego influence. See, air can move differently according to who passes by – how they move. Are they causing friction or flow? Pure thought is not a given. People are told how to behave, what to do, where to go, what to buy, etc. All this outside influence clouds the purity of thought. This produces ego. And ego rains. Ego stains. Ego moves air so that the dust settles unpredictably. Yes, dust is a metaphor. It could be a car, or the placement of a foot while walking. It can be making a very stupid decision like getting into a stranger's car. These can be considered a mistake. They are also called a lapse of judgment. But that expression implies that there was even thought behind the action. A mistake, usually happens when there IS no thought, when one is running on ego juice. So slow down a little if you want to avoid accidents, mistakes. Slow down to come closer to pure thoughts. Allow the dust to settle in a more natural way... without so much turbulence.

Impression:

She's trying to work through why she made "bad" decisions at the end of her life. She was plagued with an overactive ego.

4.21.20   Carla

There is that expression about marching to your own drummer. Society tries to get people to "march" all in line. At the same pace, in sync. This is why it is so hard to "march" alone. We are told how to be, where to go, what to wear, what to own. All of it. When you can learn to just walk alone you'll know. You'll know not only yourself but you'll know the freedom of movement that comes by moving singularly. Embrace your own way. Your own movement. There you will find a vast landscape of relief. For in moving individual you learn what YOU want, not what others tell you to want — even if they are mere suggestions. This is not to say move wildly unlike others, but just to make an attempt to do what makes you happy - do what is right for yourself. This doesn't mean be selfish. Just move to your own beat. You may sync up from time to time with others. You will see those temporary harmony movements and that will feel also like a blessing. Your truth creates your step. Step into yourself.

Impression
She tried (too) hard to be someone other than herself.
She did not lead a truthful life. She cautions us to know ourselves.

4-21-20

Carla

There is that expression about marching to your own drummer. Society tries to get people to "march" all in line. At the same pace, in sync. This is why it is so hard to "march" alone. We are told how to be, where to go, what to wear, what to own. All of it. When you can learn to just walk alone, you'll know. You'll know not only yourself, but you'll know the freedom of movement that comes by moving singularly. Embrace your own way. Your own movement. There you will find a vast landscape of relief. For in moving individually you learn what YOU want, not what others tell you to want – even if they are mere suggestions. This is not to say move wildly unlike others. But just to make an attempt to do what makes you happy – do what is right for yourself. That doesn't mean be selfish. Just move to your own beat. You may sync up from time to time with others. You will see those temporary harmonized movements and that will feel also like a blessing. Your truth creates your step. Step into yourself.

Impression:

She tried (too) hard to be someone other than herself. She did not lead a truthful life. She cautions us to know ourselves.

4.27.20   Carla

Are you making lemonade? It is time. Time to squeeze the good juices out. You know you like it, even if with sugar. It is time to do something with all those lemons. If not, they'll grow mold or turn hard. Neither of which is worth anything. So don't delay on making the best of what you already have. Often we fixate on how bitter or sour something is, yet we do nothing to either mask the flavor or try something else. If you hold on to what isn't good for you, you are weighing yourself down. Stay light, drink some refreshing juice for a new perspective. What do you do with moldy lemons? Throw them out, likely. What do you do with bad memories? Hold on to them, nearly obsess over them, when all it is is mold. Which you know can be toxic. Stop breathing mold. Clean up. Don't worry if someone or something delivers you lemons. Use them to your advantage. And if you need, just add a little water and sugar. You'll be glad you did.

Impression

Watch what you complain about in life. You have an ability to change your reaction to life's experiences.

40

4-27-20

Carla

Are you making lemonade? It is time. Time to squeeze the good juices out. You know you like it, even if with sugar. It is time to do something with all those lemons. If not, they'll grow mold or turn hard. Neither of which is worth anything. So don't delay on making the best of what you already have. Often we fixate on how bitter or sour something is, yet we do nothing to either mask the flavor or try something else. If you hold on to what isn't good for you, you are weighing yourself down. Stay light, drink some refreshing juice for a new perspective. What do you do with moldy lemons? Throw them out, likely. What do you do with bad memories? Hold on to them, nearly obsess over them, when all it is is mold. Which you know can be toxic. Stop breathing mold. Clean up. Don't worry if someone or something delivers you lemons. Use them to your advantage. And if you need, just add a little water and sugar. You'll be glad you did.

Impression:

Watch what you complain about in life. You have an ability to change your reaction to life's experiences.

5.8.20 Carla

Unliving with regret. You might think once you pass that everything is light and bliss. But that's not actually the case. At least not for me. You see, I'm living (unliving) with regret. As Carla I made bad choices. Ill choices. Unhealthy choices. Now I understand how it came to be that I made such choices. I let my ego have too much power. I was consumed with being known. Being seen. My body became my temple, but not in the sense of me taking care of it - feeding it well and exercising. I mean that my thoughts were shallow and the physical existance was the most important thing. With this ideology, I became surrounded by many people who supported my mentality. This made me feel "on top of the world." It fed my ego so my ego grew. I grew away from spirituality, from my connection to family, to my base, my ground. I was so lit up, so high in spirit (like happy) that I forgot about the other part of life. So here a I am now recognizing my "mistake" in that past life. You see, it isn't like you die and your slate is wiped clean - you live with those actions, those choices even while not living. I am here to tell you to monitor yourself, but also to share what I've learned. I can't turn back time, but I can take responsibility for where I am right now. Maybe you can do the same.

Impression

She starts to feel lighter - to understand why she is where she is. Not angry - moving into acceptance -

5-8-20

Carla

Unliving with regret. You might think once you pass that everything is light and bliss. But that's not actually the case. At least not for me. You see, I'm living (unliving) with regret. As Carla, I made bad choices. Ill choices. Unhealthy choices. Now I understand how it came to be that I made such choices. I let my ego have too much power. I was consumed with being known. Being seen. My body became my temple, but not in the sense of me taking care of it – feeding it well and exercising. I mean that my thoughts were shallow and the physical existence was the most important thing. With this ideology, I became surrounded by many people who supported my mentality. This made me feel "on top of the world." It fed my ego so my ego grew. I grew away from spirituality, from my connection to family, to my base, my ground. I was so lit up, so high in spirit (like happy) that I forgot about the other part of life. So here I am now recognizing my "mistake" in that past life. You see, it isn't like you die and your slate is wiped clean - you live with those actions, those choices even while not living. I am here to tell you to monitor yourself, but also to share what I've learned. I can't turn back time, but I can take responsibility for where I am right now. Maybe you can do the same.

Impression:

She starts to feel lighter - to understand why she is where she is. Not angry - moving into acceptance.

5.20.20   Carla

Follow the map to your heart. In other words, go inside your heart to find where you are going. Often we look for the excitement, the flair, the wild ride, figuring it will be more adventursome, provide a better story, or get us out of the bland duldrom of our life. But yet it rarely does. Usually it just keeps us away from our true end goal. Which is your own heart. Accept this, and you will find ~~ttttttt~~ more excitement in the every day. You will see the beauty in the little things in life. A cup of tea, your favorite seat, the salt shaker. With that there is no need to "get more" - there is no desire for being MORE than you already are. When you learn to accept this is when you begin to live your most fulfilled life. What are you willing to find / reveal of your own self? Will you follow the map to your heart? To what you truly love, what you most want, to what brings you joy and happiness? Can you let go of the attachments to the surface qualities and attachments in life? The "being someone" who is recognized, someone who HAS the right things, has DONE the "right" activities? Let go of what others care about and find what lights your soul.

Impression
She still has regret over her earthly actions. Wishes she would have know this lesson long ago.

44

5-20-20

Carla

Follow the map to your heart. In other words, go inside your heart to find where you are going. Often we look for the excitement, the flair, the wild ride, figuring it will be more adventuresome, providing a better story, or get us out of the bland doldrum of our life. But yet it rarely does. Usually, it just keeps us away from our true end goal. Which is your own heart. Accept this, and you will find more excitement in the every day. You will see the beauty in the little things in life. A cup of tea, your favorite seat, the salt shaker. With that there is no need to "get more" – there is no desire for being MORE than you already are. When you learn to accept this is when you begin to live your most fulfilled life. What are you willing to find, reveal of your own self? Will you follow the map to your own heart? To what you truly love, what you most want, to what brings you joy and happiness? Can you let go of the attachments to the surface qualities and attachments in life? The "being someone" who is recognized, someone who HAS the right things, has DONE the "right" activities? Let go of what others care about and find what lights your soul.

Impression:

She still has regret over her earthly actions. Wishes she would have known this lesson long ago.

7.5.20   Carla

The beauty of a Pez dispenser is that you feel like there is always another treat at the ready. And when you get to the last one you know to really savor it, while imaging the anticipation of putting in a new packet. Life can be the same way if you let it. Each event, each friend, is like a new block of Pez. Savor each one for the time it is there. And especially savor the last moments. Though in life you don't always know they are the last moments you might so with a friend, or be in a relationship, or lose something special. But when you do know, such as when you move, rember to spend equal time reminiscing as you do anticipating the new "flavor" to come. All while enjoying right where you are, who you are with, and all the experience that comes along. There are times in life when you can see a full stack before you — a series of events that will unfold. Savor each one equally In good and bad. For both are essential. If you can accept that negative things (events, people, etc) can help you, you will find your life easier to navigate and will enjoy it so much more. Go ahead, take a Pez break!

Impression
She came through easier quicker - I felt I couldn't keep up w/ what she was saying.

7-5-20

Carla

The beauty of a Pez dispenser is that you feel like there is always another treat at the ready. And when you get to the last one you know to really savor it, while imagining the anticipation of putting in a new packet. Life can be the same way if you let it. Each event, each friend, is like a new block of Pez. Savor each one for the time it is there. And especially savor the last moments. Though in life you don't always know they are the last moments you might be with a friend, or be in a relationship, or lose something special. But when you do know, such as when you move, remember to spend equal time reminiscing as you do anticipating the new "flavor" to come. All the while, enjoying right where you are, who you are with, and all the experience that comes along. There are times in life when you can see a full stack before you – a series of events that will unfold. Savor each one equally. In good <u>and</u> bad. For both are essential. If you can accept that negative things (events, people, etc.) can help you, you will find your life easier to navigate and will enjoy it so much more. Go ahead, take a Pez break!

Impression:

She came through easily and quickly - I felt I couldn't keep up with what she was saying.

9-8-20   Carla

The elements rain down on a tree, and leaves come down, too. All this is what feeds the tree to continue on. It is a cycle of rebirth each year as buds turn to leaves. You could say that the tree feeds itself if left alone with the elements. When a tree is cut down you can see its life span in the trunk. More fertile years are indicated in the rings, less fertile years show smaller growth lines. See the tree as a circle of life and also an internal cycle ⊙. It grows from itself Now apply this to your own life. You need more than water to survive. But how are your internal rings? Are the steady movements of growth? Or are they alternating between health and dispair? How are you feeding your mind, your body? See your own cycle of rebirth. See how you change — and don't change — both internally and from the outside. Do you give way for fresh buds to bloom? Do you water your foundation? Do you allow the natural elements to nourish your development?
Think on how your own cycle moves through your physical body as well as your mental capacity.
For the internal is a reflection of the outside.
And the external is a reflection of within.

<u>Impression</u>
I see a tree spiriling into itself — from the branches full of leaves into the base of the trunk, moving into the roots.

9-8-20

Carla

The elements rain down on a tree, and leaves come down, too. All this is what feeds the tree to continue on. It is a cycle of rebirth each year as buds turn to leaves. You could say that the tree feeds itself if left alone with the elements. When a tree is cut down you can see its life span in the trunk. More fertile years are indicated in the rings. Less fertile years show smaller growth lines. See the tree as a circle of life and also an internal cycle. It grows from itself. Now apply this to your own life. You need more than water to survive. But how are your internal rings? Are they steady movements of growth? Or are they alternating between health and despair? How are you feeding your mind, your body? See your own cycle of rebirth. See how you change – and don't change – both internally and from the outside. Do you give way for fresh buds to bloom? Do you water your foundation? Do you allow the natural elements to nourish your development?

Think on how your own cycle moves through your physical body as well as your mental capacity. For the internal is a reflection of the outside. And the external is a reflection of within.

Impression:

I see a tree spiraling into itself – from the branches full of leaves into the base of the trunk, moving into the roots.

10-20-20   Carla

I still feel trapped. Like locked in a room. The car. If you've ever felt trapped, even for a moment, while a door lock was jammed temporarily, you might know what I'm feeling. It becomes a feeling of suffocating. Like I'm knocking and no one is hearing. What did I do to deserve this, I keep asking myself over and over. I feel trapped with that thought - why me? What did I do? And then the useless question of what could I have done to change the outcome. Useless because it is too late now. Yet look at me, pounding on the glass — as if someone might free me from my self imposed trap. Angel, spirit, if you can hear me, please, come rescue me. I am ready to release my guilt. I am ready to break free of the chains that bind me. I am ready for the light. I will let go of the past so I can move towards the light. If only you will hear me. I will stop banging my fist on the window. I will sit here quietly until you come. I trust you will find me. Thank you.

Impression
    From frantic to calm — As if she's been in a frenzy since she passed and is ready to release it at long last. As if she needed a "time out" before she was ready to move on.

10-20-20

Carla

I still feel trapped. Like locked in a room. The car. If you've ever felt trapped, even for a moment, while a door lock was jammed temporarily, you might know what I'm feeling. It becomes a feeling of suffocating. Like I'm knocking and no one is hearing. What did I do to deserve this, I keep asking myself over and over. I feel trapped with that thought – why me? What did I do? And then the useless question of what could I have done to change the outcome. Useless because it is too late now. Yet, look at me, pounding on the glass – as if someone might free me from my self imposed trap. Angel, spirit, if you can hear me, please, come rescue me. I am ready to release my guilt. I am ready to break free of the chains that bind me. I am ready for the light. I will let go of the past so I can move towards the light. If only you will hear me. I will stop banging my fist on the window. I will sit here quietly until you come. I trust you will find me. Thank You.

Impression:

From frantic to calm – As if she's been in a frenzy since she passed and is ready to release it at long last. As if she needed a "time out" before she was ready to move on.

11-3-20   Carla

Pain is a feeling. It is also an emotion. That's why it runs so deep - why it is felt so deeply. When the outside meets the inside, there is a double feeling, a double experience. It comes across as a collision. This is one reason why people are afraid of pain. Not just because they don't want to feel it, on their body, they also don't want to have the emotional experience or reaction. This is the same with death. People are afraid of death, of dying, because of the emotional aspect of it. Of course one doesn't want to feel the pain of what comes at the last breath — whether by an accident or a result of a disease. But it doesn't have to be like this. The body might feel | less tense about pain if it feels it without bringing in the emotional aspect. How do you do that? Next time you scratch your skin, or bang your knee, or your back "hurts" — see if you can experience the pain as only a sensation. As if there is no emotion in it. Say to yourself, "this does not feel how I normally feel. I will pass through this experience and my body will return to normal." Detach yourself from putting an emphasis on the emotional feeling of pain. In this way you will have less fear about experiencing pain. Ultimately you will have less fear about dying.

Impression
  An experiment we can all relate to. Maybe it is a good idea to have pain so we can gain from the experience for other aspects of our life.

11-3-20

Carla

Pain is a feeling. It is also an emotion. That's why it runs so deep – why it is felt so deeply. When the outside meets the inside, there is a double feeling, a double experience. It comes across as a collision. This is one reason why people are afraid of pain. Not just because they don't want to feel it, on their body, they also don't want to have the emotional experience or reaction. This is the same with death. People are afraid of death, of the experience of dying, because of the emotional aspect of it. Of course, one doesn't want to feel the pain of what comes at the last breath – whether by an accident or a result of a disease. But it doesn't have to be like this. The body might feel less tense about pain if it feels it without bringing in the emotional aspect. How do you do that? Next time you scratch your skin, or bang your knee, or your back "hurts" – see if you can experience that pain as only as a sensation. As if there is no emotion in it. Say to yourself, "this does not feel how I normally feel. I will pass through this experience and my body will return to normal." Detach yourself from putting an emphasis on the emotional feeling of pain. In this way you will have less fear about experiencing pain. Ultimately, you will have less fear about dying.

Impression:

An experiment we can all relate to. Maybe it is a good idea to have pain so we gain from the experience for other aspects of our life.

11.15.20   Carla

I is the meeting of opposites. It is the coming together of two different forces. ~~XXXX~~ Where your I is made on the spectrum is different than where mine is made. When you see that I is not only individual but also made up of opposing forces finding their balance within you, you know your uniqueness. It is a pressure build-up to your own self. You do not create I-ness without these duality forces. We are all on the spectrum of love and fear. Embrace where you are. Yes, of course your location can change over time, but know you are in only one place at this exact moment. This your self placement. Only you can move yourself toward or away from love. We, a series of Is create the entire spectrum. It does not exist without each one of us on it. Don't get distracted by conceptualizing what the spectrum looks like. It is a vibration, so it FEELS. It is felt, not seen. Feel your placement. Then feel the entire spectrum. Did you know you can be connected to EVERY SINGLE person in this way? In this way you are no different than anyone else. What a beautiful idea.

Impression

I is often seen as ego. Ego separates us from others. The I she is talking about actually connects us with others. Gives us a way to feel connected to others — even people we do not know.

54

11-15-20

Carla

I is the meeting of opposites. It is the coming together of two different forces. (image) Where your I is made on the spectrum is different than where mine is made. When you see that I is not only individual but also made up of opposing forces finding their balance within you, you know your uniqueness. It is a pressure build-up to your own self. You do not create I-ness without these dualing forces. We are all on the spectrum of love and fear. Embrace where you are. Yes, of course your location can change over time. But know you are in only one place at this exact moment. This is your self placement. Only you can move yourself toward or away from love. We, a series of I's create the entire spectrum. It does not exist without each one of us on it. Don't get distracted by conceptualizing what the spectrum looks like. It is a vibration, so it FEELS. It is felt, not seen. Feel your placement. Then feel the entire spectrum. Did you know you can be connected to EVERY SINGLE person in this way? In this way you are no different than anyone else. What a beautiful idea.

Impression:

I is often seen as ego. Ego separates us from others. The I she is talking about actually connects us with others. Gives us a way to feel connected to others – even people we do not know.

1-19.21   Carla

Why do you look at me with those sad eyes? I'm ok. Yes, I do wish for some freedom, but it is my issue not yours. I think you are mirroring me, but you don't need to do that. You do you and I'll do me. You can't fix me anymore than I can fix you. Sure, we might be able to help one another, but certainly not fix... that's all about personal choices, your own decisions for how you will move about life. Just don't look at me with sadness mply to get to "read" me — just talk to me — or listen — or whatever you want. But use your OWN eyes, not mine. That's creepy, anyway. But do you hear me? Check in on your own self first. Always. Know that empathy, or caring is often a self-centered endeavor because you ASSUME you know what I'm thinking, or going through. Really, you have barely a clue, even if you might have some personal details. You are kind to care; be even kinder by being open to NOT knowing, by being open to not judging, which is how I feel when you approach me with sad eyes. Like you feel sorry for me before even asking me about how I'm doing. Tread lightly on your approach.

Impression

She's not ~~seeking~~ sympathy — she wants to take care of herself.

1-19-21

Carla

Why do you look at me with those sad eyes? I'm ok. Yes, I do wish for some freedom, but it is my issue not yours. I think you are mirroring me, but you don't need to do that. You do you and I'll do me. You can't fix me anymore than I can fix you. Sure, we might be able to help one another, but certainly not fix...that's all about personal choices, your own decisions for how you will move about life. Just don't look at me with sadness trying to get to "reach" me – just talk to me – or listen – or whatever you want. But use your OWN eyes, not mine. That's creepy, anyways. But do you hear me? Check in on your own self first. Always. Know that empathy, or caring is often a self-centered endeavor because you ASSUME you know what I'm thinking, or going through. Really, you have barely a clue, even if you might have some personal details. You are kind to care; be even kinder by being open to NOT knowing, by being open to not judging, which is how I feel when you approach me with sad eyes. Like you feel sorry for me before even asking me about how I'm doing. Tread lightly on your approach.

Impression:
She's not seeking sympathy - she wants to take care of herself.

EPILOGUE

SEE THAT YOUR LIFE IS IN YOUR HANDS. Though you come from a long line of previous "siblings" who have more impact on you than you can probably imagine, there IS an amount of freewill with which you can have some fun. But remember that your life is for a purpose. It is not to flutter away like a candy wrapper out the car window. It is serious business. Your business.

You've taken the time to read this book. Now please do the world another favor and check in with your own life purpose and decide right now, not tomorrow, and not next week sometime, to take actions that are in the best interest of your future. Even if it just keeps you out of purgatory. But consider something much more uplifted than that. Perhaps we DO have the ability to band together peacefully, arm-in-arm, and see that our potential demise is not actually necessary.

No, you cannot do it all alone, but even your consideration of it makes an impact.

Make right action today and every day. Do not forget it.

About the Author

Amelia Hathow is a recently retired elementary school teacher, who after three years studying and practicing her mediumship abilities, she wrote her first book from channeled messages she received. Her first book considers the Rapture through the story of a hunter who was killed on a hunting trip.

www.ingramcontent.com/pod-product-compliance
Lightning Source LLC
Chambersburg PA
CBHW051003140626
46546CB00017B/2748